Redbone

poems

Mahogany L. Browne

Willow Books, a division of AQUARIUS PRESS

Detroit, Michigan

Redbone

Editor: Randall Horton
Cover design: Rico Frederick

ISBN 978-0-9961390-8-3
LCCN 2015950230

INNOVATORS SERIES
WILLOW BOOKS, a division of AQUARIUS PRESS
PO Box 23096
Detroit, MI 48223

Printed in the United States of America

to Coco, for the chance to write fearlessly
to Elsie Jean, for the language & know how
to Ellaine, my mother, Redbone, for the permission

Something that can make you do wrong
Make you do right
—Al Green

Contents

Redbone Dances

If you ain't never watched your parents kiss
        ain't neva have them teach you
'bout the way lips will   to bend & curve
against a lover's affirmation

If you ain't never watched the knowing nod
of sweethearts worn away & soft
as a speakerbox's blown out hiss

If you ain't witnessed the glue
that connected your mother & father
—how they fused their single selves
into the blunt fist of parents

If you ain't sure there was a time when
their eyes held each other like a nexus
breaking the lock to dip dark marbles
into certain corners of a shot glass

If you ain't never known a Saturday night
slick with shiny promises & clouds
wrapped wet in a Pendegrass croon

If you ain't been taught how
a man hold you close   *so close*
…it look like a crawl

If you ain't had the memory
of your mother & father sliding
hip to hip   Their feet whisper
a slow shuffle & shift   Her hand
on his neck   grip the shoulder of
a man that will pass his daughters
bad tempers   & hands like bowls

If you ain't watched a man
lean into a woman His eyes
a boat sliding across bronze
          His hands
pillared in her auburn hair   Her
throat   holds   the urge
to hear how her voice sounds against
the wind of him

If your skin can't fathom the heat
of something as necessary as this...

Then you can't know the hurricane
of two bodies   how   the bodies
can create the prospect of a sunrise
how that sunrise got a name
          it sound like: a blues song;
a woman's   heart *breaking;*

From the record player   skipping
          the sky   almost
blue

Betty Sez

Betty didn't take kindly to a man's
instruction. she preferred to tell him
where to shove his opinion, instead

My great aunt was the oldest to a
brother with bricks for hands. Her glare
promised a gunbutt'n for any man that
touched her expensive handbag.

At the age of 90, she didn't hesitate to swing
Cutting the wind in half with her sinewy arms.
She snarled, he trynna steal my stuff.

She was usually right.

Redbone Wins Round 1

she twisted the bottle cap
like she wish she could twist
his neck & the argument
lasts a few minutes Before
he reaches across the room his
teeth gnarled into the soft of
his cheek the only touchable
thing she can find these days
her hands drape across her face,
        instinctively & quick,
so so quick—even still he
is quicker he thunderc l a p s
the cheekbone   the temple
the lips   bruises her
 into a rainbow woman
        stares   incredulously—
wonders how she held the glass
bottle so still–how his thunder ain't
shatter her pride into a slump
—where she found the nerve

she listens to these questions
coiling themselves around the
room drops her hands to her side
        a renewed defiancestretching
itself into the length of the kitchen
wall   she hears the silence
a mission bell   a warning alarming
the impending storm   she sets the
bottle upright on the counter ignores
the rapid tempo in her skull   hushes
away her tears   she speculates
this will end soon.

Redbone Shames the Devil

Sometimes you ain't 'posed to love up on nobody
like that. Sometimes it's too hard on the bones and
no one but your own self know what you want to do
with the weight of it all—only you know what you
can't take. Everybody told me what to do when it came
to Bam. Told me let him go. Told me leave him 'lone.
Told me take my kids and pregnant self back down
to the Valley, like there wasn't a man waiting to pull
my skin away from my scalp there, too. I tell 'em "No".
My eyes still heavy from all the sleep I ain't got and
my back on fire from the baby trying to break free
through my spine. I tell 'em "No. We goin'make this
family make sense." But what I want to say is "We goin'
fall into the night like we fell into each other and it won't
hurt no more. 'Cause I hurt when we ain't together. I hurt
'cause it remind me of the my daddy, how he make my momma
cry, how her tears carried me to sleep on the nights I forget
to close the door.

When we ain't together, I am reminded that I'm broken,
That my heart ain't got no locks 'cause it ain't got no doors
'Cause they took away my doors when I was only a baby—
Don't nobody wanna hear about a baby girl with a missing
door! That sound too much like blame. And I'm tired of how
my fingers bend and all I want is for some reason to stay
put. I want something that stay mine. My first husband
got a mean space between his chest. Took my first and second
born out of spite. He's a spiteful man. They grow in my
belly, burn my heart with pride, crush my smile into little
pieces when they cry—they was mines. And he took 'em.
He was never mines. He showed me that truth after he
ran around town in love with a newer and younger me.
My big ol' belly was just a reason enough to cheat the
first time. So by the time I got me a man, who make me feel
like I got doors on my everything, like I got a key—like I

11

control the movement in my body—I ain't care too much
that he cheat too. My husband got me used to a bed
smelling like thangs that wasn't mine. I got so used to it
by the time I met Bam I was happy someone wanted
to fight for me. I was happy even if the only person he fought
was me. Every bruise and throat clench, every grunt and
push we crater into the mattress afterwards spread through
my body warm glow bright. It matches my hair and the gap in
my teeth and it keep him coming back. Telling me sweet
everything, I don't start the mess but I ain't running to the Valley
either. Besides, he say he goin' fight the world for what's his.

I'm his. He's mines. We got this baby, too. You can't tell me that ain't
love. You can tell me anything but that…"

Betty Sez

she taught her sister-in-law three things:

1. how to cock a gun
2. how to bet on race horses & win
3. how to run, why to run, & when to stand up;
a cigarette stiff on the cliff between her lips the entire time.

Redbone Plays Bones

she got a mean side eye
got a mean hand too

you can tell how she hold
the dominoes   she been here

here: the head of the table
the driver in the passenger seat

the first   to unlock the chain in the
morning   the first to admit she mourns

almost everything   except   this
type of hand-to-hand   combat.

she tell you "dig in the graveyard"
she slur her cognac   she laugh

arched   eyebrowsmoke churns
across her face   cloaks   her restlessness

in folds of grey she asks "who you laughing at?"
in an almost serious   no one answers her

cause   she   got questions for
everything *like* it ain't her first

time hearing her own voice echo
"all the time," she say "she ain't got"

before tapping her wrist she rise
into a stumble step from the table

swing like a rag down the hall
close her door and lock it slow

a curious child jumps to   fill the empty
seat   eager to know how the graveyard

got so full. pretend such small fingers
can count losses   as quickly as   she did

slam the table   triumphantly, puncture
the air with "DOMINOE!"   before

knocking over the ashtray and her abandoned
cigarette burning down to the   filter   s l o w

Redbone in His Hands

He loved her freckles
Loved her pretty red skin
He loved her so loudly
She began to love him back

He was nicknamed after a bomb
He a quick firecracker

He was a brown bomber
All gait and guff

He slurred her name like a curse word
Slid the letter D rock slate against her neck

She loved him back harder
Loved him 'til she learned
To brace her bones against his flurry

Loved him hot and until the her
Shoulders pinned against
The floor became romantic
Loved him raw
Like a fracture & black eye blinking embers

He loved her with his hands
Never the type to leave his heart in his chest

Been buried it in his father's junkyard
Years before
He knew the slow grey hanging heavy in his breathing
Had a name

He call it   Red   Red   Red   Red
      Red   Red

Loved her freckles a swollen purple
Squeeze her hands a bear claw crunch
He loved her so much her face became a b l u r r y thing

Her glowering
amber hair
a doll's strings,
          gleaming

Just waiting
to be pulled

          out

Muddy Waters

When I think of my grandfather:

I never think of him as a fighter.
I think of his rough man hands, holding
tools, slapping five & sipping coffee

a chipped cup to his lips. Easy. Like his
smile. Like a man that loved the Blues.

I never think fist or shove or pummel.
I never think loosening teeth or bursting lips
like fruit. I only remember a kind man.

Beckoning me to the kitchen table, his legs

crossed noose-like in a pair of paint speckled
jeans. His smile, a ray of whatever brightens

the sun. He always offered me a sip of his coffee.

Sweet & mud dark.

Church Heat

Grandma Coco's church is uppity
Everyone singing like a bad opera
More white people than black folks

Redbone, Redbone Have You Heard?

Bam got tight eyes
        Real tight
He crazy, girl
        But he fun to be around
He's so funny
        He the life of the party
He the oldest of them boys over on Alcatraz
        He love them birds – the pigeons
That's what I heard
        He got a cage in the backyard
He got a cage on the roof
        He make the cage out of cardboard & wire
He scale roofs
        He think he (can) fly
I heard he stole the pigeon from Albert's coop
        All them boys went looking for Bam
He just waited for them on the stoop
        I heard they went looking through his flock
Heard they ain't found nothing
        Heard they ain't believe him
I heard his daddy made him fight them one-on-one
        Everybody know they call him Bam cause of his hands
Cause his eyes so tight & you never know when he go boom!
        He always had quick hands
That's how he call them birds back home
        The rough of his hands clapping & singing loud
That's how he fought them boys
        His hands ain't but a blur
He slap against the wind & win
        Them boys ain't never forgot
But hell, what they goin' do – he see everything
        His eyes so tight you never know what he thinking
He cracked his knuckles & they jumped on him
        He clap his hands fast & it sound like a splintered bone
They say the it sound like firecrackers

He say the birds can hear him that way
He say if he clap loud enough they know to come home
He say home with his mouth big & smiling
But his eyes never change, he's so handsome
They say that's how he knew where to hide Albert's pigeon
Say he hid Albert's bird behind the broken board
His eyes shine like crazy laughter man lightning
He got hands like his daddy
His hands are so quick
– They steal anything worth something

Betty Sez

I got a secret:

I knew I would be nobody's bride

It's better like 'dis

                                                      Besides…I ain't into taking gifts
from horses
no way.

Rita Cross Redbone

And then   there was   Rita;
a bullhorn of a woman   slick   wit Bam's
name in her mouth   from the entrance
of the corner store   she beamed   sweat
sliding down her chest   she leaned
inside the glass casing   condensation
dragging its tongue across the gold and white
cans of cheap Bud Lite   Rita called Bam's name
        thick with spit   like they   were fucking
Rita   was a piss-colored   hip heavy woman
a purple hickey sly smirking from her exposed
skin   and Redbone wasn't nothing
but another yella heffa   out to get her man   Rita
laughed her tongue   poked out   like a child
she tapped her finger   against the taut skin of her
growing belly   held Bam's arm tight with the other
red fingernails   *pinchandrelease* pinch   and
pinch again   to make sure   he was real – and hers
like the last white teddy bear   from a street fair full
of dust   Bam   didn't look at her   once
  she shifted her foot   and smiled   tight

The Big House

Rita moved into the Big House on Alcatraz and winked like a fox
in a chicken coop at the fading mirage of Redbone. She patted her
belly, smiled at his mother, cooed at his father like a blues juke
joint brewed in her blood. She sat on the stoop of Alcatraz, the
biggest house painted like the sky, sitting spread eagle in the middle
of Berkeley's intersection. The Big House was named after the
penitentiary reckless enough to have its own island. Rita sat on the
sprawling white teeth of the stairs and dreamed. She dreamed there
was no color red -- only Bam and Rita and babies. She dreamed she
was always pregnant and the walls caved in and curved out. She
dreamed the waves of babies flushed themselves in reverse from her
past mistakes and into her patient arms. Her breasts swelled warm
with the idea. The heat unfolded in her chest dashed quickly across
her sternum before spreading dense through her belly. The fire
rumbled through her body causing a wretched tear to shoot from her
throat. She lay her head, heavy and spinning, on the white wood and
felt the hot rush, like the Oakland Hills brushfire, dance around her
belly and settle calmly in her lap. Her eyes flickered. She could only see
the babies, all of the tight-eyed babies surrounding her feet, she was
too busy dreaming to notice all the blood.

RedBone in Greek

First Husband walk in
Let the light vanish
Whole room close like fist
Squeeze air from throat
Redbone legs shake
But Redbone eyes ain't move
Redbone whisper
"I make him stone He can't hurt me, I make him stone"
Her eyes become graveyards
Redbone's First Husband ain't but a man to Medusa
Redbone don't move
Don't give him reason to take first and second born
Again
Redbone & First Husband watch children fiddle
With empty space of the apartment
Redbone watch First Husband stalk around room
First Husband dust every corner with cobalt eyes
Redbone chant in her head "I make him stone He can't hurt me,
I make him stone I make him stone I make him..."
Redbone heart turn trampoline
Redbone heart ain't never beat for First Husband
Like this
Redbone think "Love funny that way"
Redbone smirk *"I do not love him, I make him stone, I have never*
Loved him like this, I make him stone, I make him stone, I make him.."
First Husband frown like he can hear what Redbone thinking
First Husband walk to front door & growl "I'll be back Sunday"
Redbone palm swat door close
"I make him stone, I make him stone, I make him stone"
Redbone sniff sweet sweat of her breath
& cry

Redbone on Snapping Peas

It broke my heart, when they moved Rita
in that house. The house where I snapped
peas with his mama and his sister. My
skin just itch thinking 'bout Rita and her
big ole' hips up in there like she kin. Like
she family. She steady say she pregnant.
Just'a twisting her neck every time I come
'round Alcatraz. Like she own the porch or
something, like a yella girl need be afraid
of her 'bama-ass glare. That's why I tell him,
"you betta go get your girl" he say "you IS
my girl" I say "naw, ya' **girl** is in ya mama
house snapping peas!" He smile big, so big
his eyes close and grab my arm real tight
—like he can't let go even if he wanted to.
And I pretend I can't stand him when really
I just can't breathe. He too close. I can smell
the sun on his brown skin and I get jealous.
So I snatch away from him like my arm on
fire and start with the excuses "I got to work"
or "I got to meet my cousin" or "I'm 'bout to
go see my ex-husband" and Oooh! He hate
that last one. His eyes dance at me sharp
daggers, like he wronged or something! Like
I'm the one with a woman claiming my first
born. His eyes go real dark and flare like
a burning bush. My arm still hot from his
touch. And he on me. His skin touching mine.
His arms everywhere and I won't let go. I try
to think of anything But his eyes, his hands…
I try to stop loving him. Tried to stop thinking
'bout his smile and how he smile bright as
the blackest sky. How he in my dreams just
running round causing me grief, giving me
indigestion, making me lose sleep. Thinking

26

'bout Bam keep my toes curling all on they own
when he call me "Red" and slur "girl" like he
hiding a Mississippi sharecropper in his throat.
He say my name like it's his favorite word like
a man in love with the way I sound on his tongue,
for a minute I forget all of it. I forget about Rita
and the son she done promised him, the kitchen
table with the matching white chairs and them
snapping peas—I swear I can only feel the earth
moving underneath us. Even after I climb into
the car and roll the window all the way down,
my arm stinging bright with his fingerprints on top.

Redbone and the Rabbit Fur Coat

When she went to the nightclub with Natasha
wearing a rabbit fur coat like a swan's neck
her face awash in foundation & sparkles
her smile glittered in the night

       all he saw was her fleeing like a race car
              red top on fire & dancing in the distance
       all he saw was her ghost moving
              bouncing raggedy against the night's air
       all he saw was her perfume bottle toppled over
              a drunken bucket rinsing the raised wood
       all he saw was her cheeks tight with laughter
              striking the jagged bell of single woman's glee

When she went to the nightclub with Natasha
she returned with wine on her tongue & warm hands
her face was slick with sweat from the dank disco room
her smile forgetting their fight, his absence, his snarl

      all he saw was her shoulders square & sharp
           a rigged knife, an envious steak alive in his chest
      all he saw was her hair ruffled & untamed
           the curls sweeping across her forehead like a church hymn
      all he saw was her mouth, a shovel collapsing into the red earth
           a cursed gift, wrapped loosely by another man's voice
      all he saw was red
           her hair, her skin, her blood

When she went to the nightclub with Natasha
she danced alone to the songs she knew best
she filled the room with the noise of her hips
softly mouthed the words as if she was held her hostage

      all he saw was the rabbit fur coat
            brown patches lingering against her arms
      all he saw was the rabbit fur coat
            patches of brown just daring him to snatch them clean
      all he saw was her open hands, outstretched fingers
            raised heaven high as if she were drowning
      all he saw was his fists machete across the living room's sky
            diving into her softest parts, like a sickle moon

Bam be like…

Redbone was something else

MANNNNNNNN
she kept me on my toes, boy
she caught me cheating on her
drove me to ole' girl house

& said

"tell that bitch you coming home"

Redbone & Al Green

Love & Happiness
on vinyl just sound better.

Listen to this song…
Al sound like he miss
his Lady bad, don't he?

Listen.

I can't stand to hum along
to man with a hole in his heart.

Redbone's Flour Doll

Your daddy loved to show you off.
When he saw you he couldn't resist.
He would toss you in the air
like some damn sack of flour, you
look like a brown baby doll all
flowered in white ruffles &   flying.

Church Heat

Not enough folk that know how to neatly braid a little brown girl's hair

Jaundice

You came differently, thrashing your limbs until the blood spilled clean
Sun ain't even set before Bam claimed "she got my smile"—I thought he said "spine"
A disaster always got a woman's name attached to its entrance
You come justa howlin'—a yellow baby born too soon

The sun ain't even set before Bam claimed "she got my smile"—I thought he said "spine"
They say this is how the walls sweat with sin when a woman speaks
You come justa howlin'—a yellow baby born too soon
When you squealed a welcome song, I knew you'd be the thunder in my throat

They say this is how the walls sweat with sin when a woman speaks
Say her mouth is her greatest weapon & her tongue be a grenade pin dangling
When you squealed a welcome song, I knew you'd be the thunder in my throat
Knew I'd stretch my sound across an Oakland intersection to save your adorn & tick

Say her mouth is her greatest weapon & her tongue be a grenade pin dangling
Bam was a thief. He stole my sunshine when I threatened to change the locks on my heart
Knew I'd stretch my sound across an Oakland intersection to save your adorn & tick
Eclipsed your smile under the safest parts of Oklahoma & promised to kill you before Spring

Bam was a thief. He stole my sunshine when I threatened to change the locks on my heart
I got tired of his hands stealing my memories. He got tired of my weapon getting in the way
Eclipsed your smile under the safest parts of Oklahoma & promised to kill you before Spring
You twister toxemia child—I knew you would be the rebirth of a different me

I got tired of his hands stealing my memories. He got tired of my weapon getting in the way
You came differently, thrashing your limbs until the blood spilled clean
You twister toxemia child—I knew you would be the rebirth of a different me
A disaster always got a woman's name attached to its entrance

Redbone & Box Wine

You were the hardest to raise—
you just needed too much. By
the time you was thirteen maybe
fourteen-years-old, I was done
being somebody's Mama. I had
us a nice place, a desk job for the
State, I had me some friends with
no drama. Just music & Kool's
Playing cards & box wine. You like
to drive me crazy always asking
'bout Bam, where & when he
coming to visit…If he goin' send
more of them earrings in the broken
china box that turn ya ears all types
of nasty colors. I still don't know
where they came from—but I know
when I smell another woman on the
fire red plastic…But hell, I let you be.
You ain't got much to remember him
By no how. But you got his eyes,
girl… Yea, them all his.

Church Heat III

The double doors close out the summer breeze
The women in their choir robes, swaying with eyes closed
Was the reason Grandma Coco rose early on Sundays
Was the reason she bellowed her tenor bell
Was the place she prayed for Redbone
Like she paid the light bill

Redbone on Fighting

When she come to grab
you, pick up a garbage
can & work that big ass girl.
Swing on her like you did
your brother when he
ripped your favorite book.
Don't cry – swing! Hell,
I already knew she was trouble...
Don't nobody with good sense
forget to close the screen door.

Bam Behind Bars after Beating a Man with a Baseball Bat

"I let him live,   didn't I?"

Love Song

For Elsie Jean & Pau

i never heard my grandmother

say "i love you" to my grandfather.

my grandfather would sooner say he

loved us ashy brown pawn pieces &

"children, your grandma just mean"

he'd smile with an honesty weeping

from his wrinkles.

my grandmother, a brownstone dish

hand crossed southern full of prim,

proper & hot water cornbread—

would pay him no mind. her neck

a swivel swing cracked his old man

banter & she could ignore him like

the loudest sirens serenading an oakland

sky on friday.

      "i ain't stutin' you"

she waved, kitchen spoon, swimming

gravy or collard greens. her hips

swayed along to the rhythm under

her breath. his eyes danced along

she pretended like she know

he was checkin' for her beat.

later, the cancer ate through his

bones like chalk she stay oiling

his flaking skin & scrubbing the walls

with Clorox   she stay humming a song

through the nights   his lungs   lurched

for air   only her hips & his ears

 knew the words.

Redbone & The Cop

he got a motorcycle, its loud,
if you ride it up Greenhaven Avenue
it make your whole body tingle.

he got a gun & he smell like
sour smells. he stomp around
Redbone new house like he owns it.

Redbone is a porcelain doll,
she wait for him to say words
that form sentences. he do.

but when he don't, he just sit
in a grey cloud of sizzle & steel.
Redbone sit there, too. waiting
for something to happen.

The Cycle

Break womb
Break glass
       Break
       Break
    Break
Break

    Red cries
    Red plans
    Red sighs
    Break

Bam lies
Bam knows
Bam leaves
Break

    Red lives
    Red laughs
    Red learns
    Break

Red open
Red wide
Red broken
Break

    Red baby
    Red husband
    Red lonely
    Break

Red lonely

Red runs
Red hides
Red unpacks
Break

Red runs
Red unpacks
Red hides
Break

Red sun
Red shines
Red loves
Break

Red believes
Red holds
Red regrets
Break

Red weeps
Red recovers
Red conceals
Break

Red lost
Red found
Red footing
Break

Red falls

Red baby   Red smoke
Red leaves   Red lies
Break   Break

                                                      Red beat
                                                      Red down
                                                      Red fly y y y y
                                                      Crack
                                                                    Crack
                                                             Crack

                                                                    Cr
                                                                    a/
                                                                    ck

What We Lost in the Fire

she done
gone lost her mind
gone black blank
rubble rubbish
piles and piles
of smoke
       clear caved in chest
      spread beds burn
            before ashes spread
                  down 95 south
in a land of Mary
in a land of black and merry
in a land
      where Redbone found
       clouds to
       corner her
       like he did --
          once
she fled for her baby and her *baby's* baby
she think smoke can't find them there
too // like she can't see the clouds thick with
almost   when it spread way up North
UP near the boulevard   where a planet
cradle the biggest stones for home   here
her baby   and her *baby's* baby find a lullaby
in the belly of a steel horse Redbone so hungry for hustle
gristle crack break *baby's* jaw run slack her child
boomerang dey mama's sunshine to a southern city
with a cardinal's nest for a name Redbone find smoke there
too//   where the smoke is less grey almost white
so white   she dream of clouds   again
      dream of arms full of her *baby's* baby
      she is always a
fragment of a coast-sludged woman
      she is always a mother

heaving grief the size of her only name
      she be:
      missing her own mother
      swaddled in smoke and guilt

—it kills everything:
              a people
              a home
              or a spirit—*yea*
guilt can kill a spirit
too//

Church Heat

Grandma Coco love her church
Love her church friends & them boring sermons
Love to bring her grandbabies, dull eyes shining
Love to see they dresses clean
& coarse curls pinned up on each side

Birth Rite

Bam's first daughter
wears the crown
of the son he always wanted

she play basketball
with men that smell
like his shadow

her bones gather
into a huddle of chaos
she palms the sky

she s t r e t c h across
the blacktop   the sky pull
at her jaws until her lips feel

the sharp of teeth   she
growl like him they say
she decide it is her favorite sound

Bam be like...

don't put no gangbanger in here with me
      Why you shaking your head?
don't put no funny boys up in here neither
      Why you shaking your head?
send me a letter
      Why you shaking your head?
don't send me no letter...
      ...Then I don't have no daughter

Redbone Reflection

i.

* yo, read my palm
let us find wisdom in the wine
in time, the wine will make us lovewise

* i am a product of the dirt, love
the love produces dirt, creates we
we create destructive circles in cycles:
a cesarean in reverse

*an addict with an addiction to the addicted
an addiction to addicts ain't as sexy as it seems
children born in this kind of desert
are always thirsty

ii.
give me my mother's bone structure
& her gap tooth slaughter
give me her spine --RedBone got a spine for the world
give me a vertebrae for him to lose his religion in
give him a way to find my lost a way back home

iii.

a man without a god is:

a bear trap

a glorious disaster

a beautiful hemorrhage

*****

a woman without a god is:
an offering of the sweetest ache
the reddest blood; a leaking tease 'til
the hottest part of a jealous sun
blink its burnt out husk

goodnight

Redbone in God's Image

Redbone live across the street from the mall now
She used to have a BMW, she used to have a husband,
She used to own a house,
With kids in the front room & a crack habit
That got too big to hide in a valley's cul de sac

She say she clean now
She say she top heavy & in God's image
She say *"we blessed, tho, we sure are blessed
to be here"* --Coco's descendants

She say she live by the 99 cent store now
She say she need the Obama phone
She say, I live by the mall, everything is around here
She say *"I'm good with that"*

Church Heat

She ain't notice how they slouch in they seats
How they hands dog-eared the church's new bibles
How they sat with tights corkscrewed at the ankles,
Swallowing hem lines whole

My Mother, Redbone

ain't no wonder my curves curse a song
BLACK girls be full of dirt
carnation milk and tidal waves

my mother, Redbone,
split into twos for her lovers
birthed a trifecta of globes for them fools

my mother ain't neva pray with me.

Redbone ain't no heathen
just a *fire*tongue slow *c r a w l* woman

she taught me to hiss my simmer s l o w

Redbone a mighty tool
a firestack, smoking—
a bow missing every arrow
like an itchy trigger finger

her cackle break through the wind like law
Redbone ain't neva been afraid of a gut check

don't speak 'bout paperbags
Redbone cackle her words
lick the wind like law
  you minez
all BLACK all tidal waves
you'za pretty ol' downpour

my mother ain't neva pray with me

Redbone sock baby girl name to the sky

Redbone get tough quick or
get ghost quicker

Redbone sip her simmer hiss talk s l o w

Redbone's baby girl become BLACK girl

BLACK GIRL wonder why her
skin tug loose—nightfall rain

ain't no need askin' forgiveness
for what the D'vil done already let loose.

I am her greatest weapon

TO DO LIST

you don't just leave
you don't just sit
you don't just walk
you don't talk back
you don't smoke in the house
you don't scream when it hurt
you don't let them know it hurt
you don't give the scream a sound
you don't pray no more
you don't church on sundays
you don't pretend you care
you smoke wherever you want/you smoke everywhere/you don't keep a
glass of water near/you let it all burn/you let it all burn/you bury the secrets
in smoke/ you let it all burn/you let it all burn/you let it all burn/you let it all
burn/until it get clean

This

this kin this stone toss family   this kin this death of choice   this choice of addiction
this kin addicted to dying   this black death that smells like home   this home
this heart has no home   this heart found a home in Brooklyn   in airports   in a
little girl's smile in the halo of gentrification   in a little bit better   it will
all be better   if I could just have this home   this house   this man that i love
this love i can't hold   this man that i need   this life i can't hold   this want   this
now   this here   sprawled inside my chest   this black   that I can't sepa-
rate from my skin   this bone   attached to the breaking sunrise of this   smile
this root of all evil   this woman   this evil this woman   this God   this evil
to think myself evil   this God   this evil to think myself   anything less than
        woman:
        this Bermuda
        this Stonehenge
        this temple
        this flesh & this fat
        this sister
        this lover
        this wife

this *here*   be more than jump off   this be more than your free milk
this be your mother's lonely   this black girl   this bricklayer
this woman
that can't forget how to kiss like shadows how to smile like crypt keepers how to pray like a
whisper how to forget where she came from   where she came from?   from a gutter
of a woman   & a jawbreaker of a man   this hammer head love   sits on my
chest
this crunch   this crush   this sound of breakable things   this worthless thing
this worthwhile thing   this breath is worthwhile   this hurt is worth now   this
now is worth tomorrow this tomorrow ain't even here yet this concrete crack tomorrow
this glass chipped tomorrow   this morning song of good   this Billie Holiday heart-
break *good*   this Nina Simone *feel good*   tomorrow's full of good

        & heart clatter/& it sound like love/this love/this harbor/this boat/this water/this
love

        this faith/this cliff/this dive/this miss & dive again, still/this love /that loves much

more than love/this girl/that loves a love like this/this sinner's smile/this jack
knife   heart/this blade rebirth/this pulse/ with a face like our own
        this bloody pulp

this

        this

About the Author

The Cave Canem and Poets House alumn is the author of several books including *Dear Twitter: Love Letters Hashed Out On-line*, recommended by Small Press Distribution & About.com's *Best Poetry Books of 2010*. Mahogany bridges the gap between lyrical poets and literary emcee. Browne has toured Germany, Amsterdam, England, Canada and recently Australia as 1/3 of the cultural arts exchange project Global Poetics. Her journalism work has been published in the magazines *Uptown, KING, XXL, The Source, Canada's The Word* and UK's *MOBO*. Her poetry has been published in the literary journals *Pluck, Manhattanville Review, Muzzle, Union Station Mag, Literary Bohemian, Bestiary, Joint* & *The Feminist Wire*. She has several new poetry collections: *Smudge* (Button Poetry), *Redbone* (Willow Books) & the anthology *The Break Beat Poets: New American Poetry in the Age of Hip-Hop* (Haymarket). She is an Urban Word NYC mentor, as seen on HBO's Brave New Voices and facilitates performance poetry and writing workshops throughout the country. Browne is also the publisher of Penmanship Books, the Nuyorican Poets Café Poetry Program Director and Friday Night Slam curator and currently an MFA Candidate for Writing & Activism at Pratt Institute.

Grateful acknowledgement is made to the editors of the following publications where these poems first appeared: *No, Dear*: "Redbone Reflection," *The Manhattanville Review*: "What We Lost in the Fire," *Union Station Magazine*: "Redbone & Al," & "Redbone, Redbone Have You Heard," & *Muzzle Magazine*: "The Big House."

Many thanks for the heartache and headache to my family: J. & Amari, Nicole Sealey & the Cave Canem family, *Redbone: Biomythography* Cast: Mel Hsu, Orlando Hunter & Leslie Lissaint; Eboni Hogan, Falu, Randall Horton, Heather Buchanan & Willow Books.